When Mom or Dad Dies

A Book of Comfort for Kids

Written by Daniel Grippo
Illustrated by R.W. Alley

ONE
CARING
PLACE

Abbey Press
St. Meinrad, IN 47577

To my parents and parents everywhere
who faithfully nurture the lives entrusted to them.

Text © 2008 Daniel Grippo
Illustrations © 2008 Saint Meinrad Archabbey
Published by One Caring Place
Abbey Press
St. Meinrad, Indiana 47577

Library of Congress Catalog Number
2008925910

ISBN 978-0-87029-415-0

Printed in the United States of America

A Message to Parents, Teachers, and Other Caring Adults

Parents bring children into the world intending to care for them and watch them grow to adulthood. From their earliest days, children turn to their parents for a sense of safety and security in the world. All of this is turned upside down when a parent dies.

This book brings a message of understanding, comfort, and hope to children at this difficult time. They miss Mom or Dad terribly, and they don't understand why this happened. They feel strange at home, at school, among friends, but most of all inside. Painful feelings well up and it's hard for a child to know what to do with them.

How can caring adults help? We can encourage grieving children to talk about their feelings. We can listen with compassion to what they say, without judging or saying "should" and "should not" about the way they feel. We can give them the time and space they need to adjust to life without Mom or Dad.

When a parent dies, an entire family grieves. If you are the surviving parent, your challenge is great indeed—how to allow yourself to grieve while still being there for your kids? Drawing closer as a family and letting your children see you grieving will give them permission to express their own grief. Read through this book together as a place to start.

As friends and neighbors, we can encourage other kids to be considerate of grieving children but also to stay close to them and not isolate them. We can help the hurting family in practical ways—bringing a casserole by the house or offering a hand with the yard work. Teachers can make sure grieving children receive a little extra attention and assistance with homework. School counselors can encourage children to talk about their feelings.

If we pull together at this time of sorrow and loss, grieving children will come through the experience knowing that they are cared for and loved. They will be able to live the full and happy life their Mom or Dad still wants for them.

—Daniel Grippo

Home Doesn't Feel Right

Mom or Dad has died and home isn't the same. It used to be the place you felt really good, all cozy and comfortable, a warm and happy place. But now it's a sad and quiet place. There's an empty place at the table every time you sit down to eat.

Your whole family misses Mom or Dad a lot. But one thing you can do for each other is to stay close as a family. You need each other right now, and you all understand how hard it is. Give everyone in your family a big hug today.

Friends Treat You Differently

Your friends might not come around to visit as much, and they might be real quiet when they are with you for a while. They probably don't know what to say or do. Don't worry—they still like you and want to be your friends. They just want to give you some time.

You can tell them that you still want to be their friend, too. When the time is right, maybe you'll want to talk to a really good friend about how you feel.

Your Life Has Changed

When Mom or Dad died, a lot of things changed. Maybe Mom used to do most of the shopping, or Dad liked to cook. Now maybe you have to do the laundry or mow the grass.

Sure, you'd like to be playing with your friends instead of doing extra chores around the house, but you can look at the extra chores as a way to remember your Mom or Dad in a special way. They really did a lot of things for you, stuff you never really thought about. Helping out around the house is a way you can say "Thanks" to them.

Special Days Feel Strange

Some of your favorite days might be some of your saddest days this year. You may not feel very happy at the holidays. Your birthday won't be the same without Mom or Dad there when you blow out the candles.

You can make some changes in the way you celebrate special days. You might even decide as a family to go on a holiday trip together. In years to come, these days can become days when your family remembers Mom or Dad in a special way, maybe sharing stories and favorite memories.

Elf
Lake
Resort

It's Okay to Feel Sad

You miss Mom or Dad a lot, and sometimes that makes you feel really sad. You might be in a store and see something that reminds you of Dad, or be playing in the park when you remember how Mom used to take you there. These are good memories but sometimes they hurt.

You will feel like crying sometimes, and that's okay. Crying helps us feel better when we are sad. You don't have to hide your tears. Make sure you get all the hugs you need when you feel sad.

Are You Lonely?

There are times when you probably feel all alone. Maybe at night you miss Mom or Dad tucking you in or reading to you. Sometimes the house might seem really empty and lonely.

What can you do when you feel lonely? You can call and invite a good friend to come over to play for a while. Maybe your grandparents can come over for a visit or you can spend the weekend at their house. They miss your Mom or Dad, too, and will take extra good care of you when you visit.

What to Do When You're Mad

Do you sometimes get really angry about what happened? It wasn't fair that Mom or Dad died, and that makes you mad. You can't bring them back, and that makes you mad, too. What should you do?

It's okay to feel mad, but try not to hurt anyone with your anger by yelling or hitting or being mean. Instead, go outside and run and jump and play until you are out of breath and feel really tired. Then you can calm down and think about the things that make you angry, and you can talk to someone who will understand.

Maybe You're Scared

The world sometimes feels like a scary place since Mom or Dad died. Maybe you're afraid you will die, too. After all, if someone as big as Mom or Dad could die, you could, too, right?

The truth is, you can expect to grow up and live a long and healthy life. You will always have people in your life who love you and care about you. When you are scared, let your loved ones know how you feel, so they can help you feel safe again.

It Wasn't Your Fault

When someone we love dies, sometimes we feel guilty, like it was "our fault" that they died. But that's not true—you didn't want Dad or Mom to die, and you didn't make it happen by being "bad."

Even if Mom or Dad had to yell at you sometimes to pick up your room or turn the music down, that had nothing to do with their dying. There's no reason to blame yourself or anyone for what happened, because that won't help you feel better.

Why Did It Happen?

You have a lot of questions. Why did Mom or Dad die? Where did they go? When will I see them again? It would be nice if we had answers to all our questions about death, but we don't. Not even the grown-ups in your life have all the answers.

But even though we don't have all the answers, we have each other, and we have God, who made and cares for us all, in heaven and on earth. Stay close to your family, and with time, you will discover the answers to your questions.

God Is Also Your Parent

Your Mom or Dad will always love you, but so does God, who is the Parent of us all. God is with you at this hard time in your life, and God will be with you always. God loves you and cares for you, and also loves your Mom or Dad.

You can talk to God any time you want to, because God is always listening. You can talk to God about how much you miss Mom or Dad, and ask God to watch over them and over you, too.

You Can Talk About It

When you are sad, scared, lonely, mad, or just confused about what happened to Dad or Mom, you can talk about it. There are people who care about you and want to help you. It's good to talk a lot about what you are feeling, because that will help you understand things and feel better. You will feel lighter and brighter and more hopeful after you talk about how you feel.

Don't be shy or afraid to let your loved ones know how you really feel. They will listen and understand.

You Can Remember

What are some of the nice things you can do to remember your Dad or Mom? Maybe you can take some of their photos, cards, and notes and put them in a nice scrapbook. You can keep it for a long time and look at it any time you want.

Your Mom or Dad probably taught you valuable lessons like how good it is to share with others. You can remember them in a special way by doing what they taught you—like sharing with someone a toy or gift Mom or Dad gave you.

You Can Be Happy Again

It's okay to play again, to laugh again, to have fun again. That's what your Mom or Dad wants for you. They want you to be happy, to grow up and learn many things. They want you to live a full life of faith, hope, and love. That's what all the people who love and care for you also want for you.

Being a loving person is the best way you can say "THANK YOU!" in big letters to your Mom or Dad for all they have done for you. It is a big Thank-You Card you can send Mom or Dad every single day.

Daniel Grippo is a spirituality writer and editor with 30 years' experience in religious publishing. He is co-publisher of TrueQuest Communications in Chicago, www.truequest.biz.

R. W. Alley is the illustrator for the popular Abbey Press adult series of Elf-help books, as well as an illustrator and writer of children's books. He lives in Barrington, Rhode Island, with his wife, daughter, and son. See a wide variety of his works at: www.rwalley.com.